UNITED STATES
SUPREME COURT
LIBRARY

Byron White

by Bob Italia

Published by Abdo & Daughters, 6535 Cecilia Circle, Edina, Minnesota 55439.

Copyright © 1992 by Abdo Consulting Group, Inc., Pentagon Tower, P.O. Box 36036, Minneapolis, Minnesota 55435. International copyrights reserved in all counties. No part of this book may be reproduced in any form without written permission from the publisher. Printed in the United States.

Photo credits: A/P Wide World Photos-6, 13, 14, 18
                      Archive Photos-10
                      FPG International-35
                      UPI/Bettmann-cover, 5, 11, 17, 21, 22

Edited by: Paul Deegan

Library of Congress Cataloging-in-Publication Data

Italia, Robert, 1955-
      Byron White / written by Bob Italia ; [edited by Paul Deegan].
         p. cm. — (Supreme Court justices)
      Includes index.
      Summary: A career biography of Supreme Court Associate Justice Byron White.
      ISBN 1-56239-095-3
      1. White, Byron R., 1917- —Juvenile literature. 2. Judges—United States—
Biography—Juvenile literature. [1. White, Byron R., 1917- . 2. Judges. 3. United
States. Supreme Court—Biography.] I. Title. II. Series.
KF8745.W48I86 1992
347.73'2634—dc20
[B]
[347.3073534]
[B]

                                     92-13714
                                          CIP
                                          AC

Table of Contents

The "Whiz" of the Supreme Court

Byron R. "Whizzer" White is one of the oldest United States Supreme Court Associate Justices. Yet despite his age, the 74-year-old justice remains one of the

Justice White and his family.

youngest-thinking minds on the Court. He is known for his tough and aggressive questioning of lawyers. And he won't hesitate to challenge his law clerks to an intellectual debate.

White has been involved in some of the most emotionally charged cases of our day. His rulings, though usually not earth-shattering, are intelligent and consistent. And he has served as a balancing force between liberal and conservative justices.

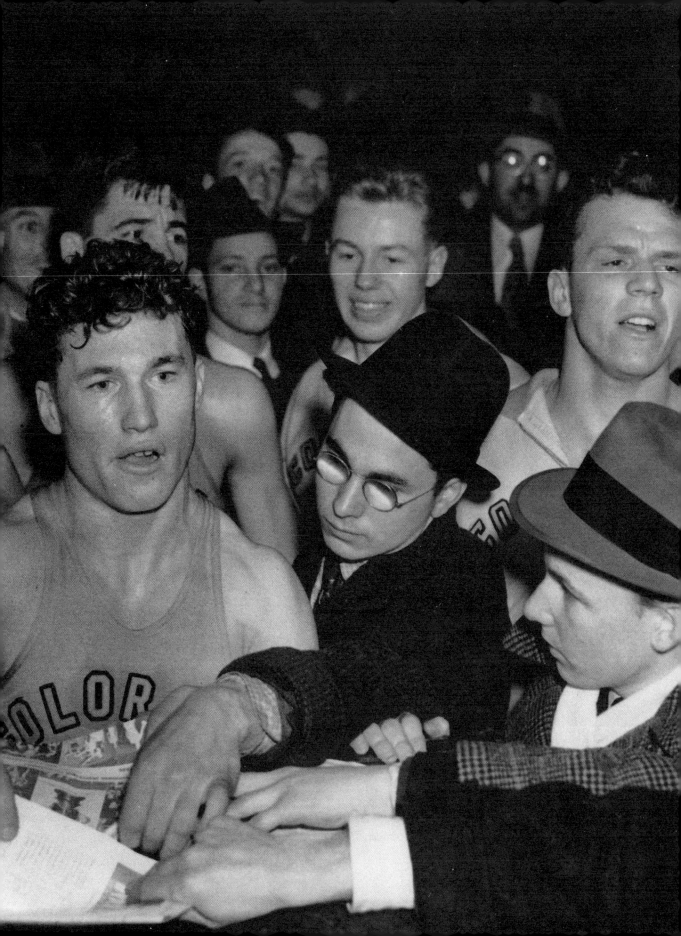

Born into the World of Politics

Born in 1917 in Fort Collins, Colorado, Byron White immediately entered the world of politics. His father, Alfred White, was a lumber dealer. He was also a staunch Republican and mayor of Wellington, Colorado.

White was a hard working young man. While in high school, he first worked in the nearby sugar beet fields, then as a railroad section hand.

Byron White (far left) on the University of Colorado basketball team.

White was also a gifted athlete, blessed with great speed and quickness. He was a star halfback on the University of Colorado football team. Because he was so fast, White was given the nickname "Whizzer"—a name that would stick with him the rest of his life.

During his senior year, White led Colorado to an undefeated regular season and a post-season trip to the Cotton Bowl. He was runner-up for the Heisman Trophy as the country's outstanding college football player. White led the nation in scoring, rushing, and total offense. In addition to his football success, White played on Colorado's baseball and basketball teams.

Rushing for the NFL

White received a Rhodes Scholarship after graduating from Colorado. He planned to study law at Oxford University in England. But a professional football team, the Pittsburg Pirates (now known as the Pittsburg Steelers) of the National Football League, offered White $15,800 to play for them. No one in pro football made that much money. White could not turn down the offer.

"How can I refuse an offer like that?" he said at the time. "It will pay my way through law school."

That year, 1938, White led the NFL in rushing. Once the football season ended, White entered Oxford University. But he did not stay long. World War II had just broken out in Europe, and White was forced to return to the United States.

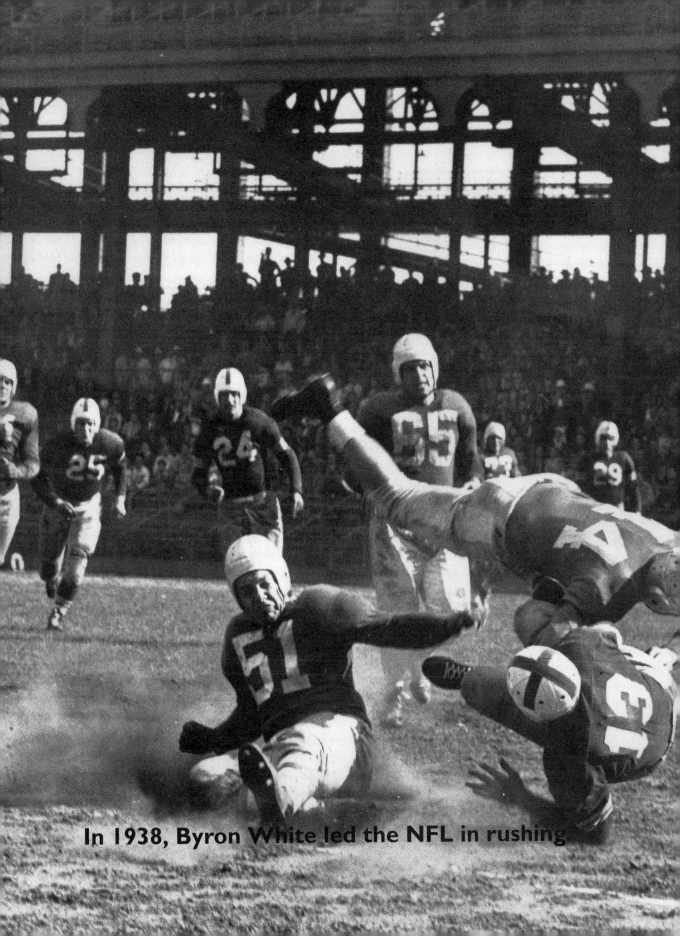

In 1938, Byron White led the NFL in rushing

White Meets John F. Kennedy

Before he left Europe, White made a very important contact. It would one day help place him on the Supreme Court. White met John F. Kennedy, the son of America's Ambassador to Great Britain. White impressed young Kennedy. Years later Kennedy, as President of the United States, would remember White when there was a vacancy on the Supreme Court.

Byron White pictured in the Solomon Islands, where he served in the Navy during World War II.

White returned to the United States in 1940. He enrolled in Yale Univeristy to study law. He also decided to play professional football for the Detroit Lions. That year, "Whizzer" White once again led the NFL in rushing.

In 1942, after the United States entered World War II, White joined the Navy. Eventually he was promoted to lieutenant.

In 1943, White was sent to the Solomon Islands in the South Pacific. There he served as a naval intelligence officer. He also was reunited with John F. Kennedy. Now a war hero, Kennedy had just survived a harrowing experience fighting the Japanese while aboard the famous Navy torpedo boat, PT 109.

White poses in front of the Supreme Court building following his appointment as law clerk to Chief Justice Vinson.

After the war, White returned to Yale University to finish his law studies. Not surprisingly, White graduated magna cum laude which is a very high honor. Immediately, White was selected to be a law clerk for Fred Vinson, the Chief Justice of the United States Supreme Court. White renewed his friendship with John Kennedy, who was now a Congressman from Massachusetts.

When his clerkship was over, White returned to Colorado. There he worked for a law firm in Denver that specialized in corporate law. White spent thirteen years at the firm and stayed away from the political scene. His only involvement came as an occasional Democratic party worker.

Campaigning for a President

White's political involvement changed in a big way prior to the 1960 elections. John F. Kennedy was running for president. White wanted to do all he could for his longtime friend. White headed the Colorado Democratic party's effort to get

John F. Kennedy (r) was greeted by White upon his arrival in Colorado in 1959.

Kennedy the party's nomination for president. White worked long and hard for Kennedy. Eventually, 27 of Colorado's 42 Democratic convention delegates sided with Kennedy.

At the convention, Kennedy received the Democratic nomination. White worked with Robert F. Kennedy, who was John Kennedy's younger brother and campaign manager, on the election campaign. White was in charge of "Citizens for Kennedy," a group that gathered the voting support of non-Democrats. In November 1960, Kennedy defeated Richard M. Nixon in a close election.

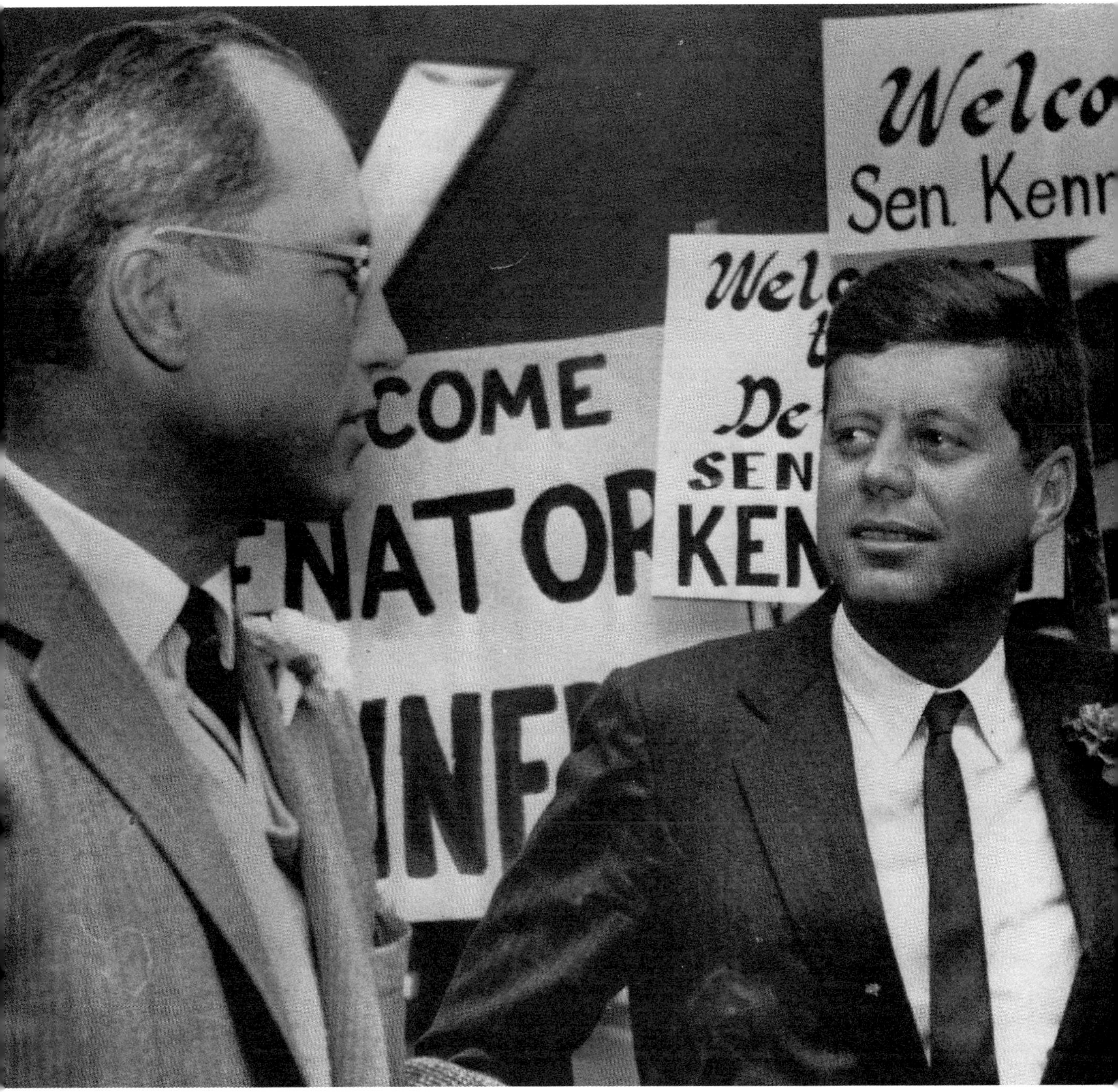
Welco
Sen. Kenn
COME
ENATOR
SEN
KEN

The new President named Robert Kennedy Attorney General. The Kennedys then chose Byron White to be Deputy Attorney General. White was the second most powerful man in the Justice Department.

As Deputy Attorney General, White handled civil rights and antitrust cases. (Antitrust laws forbid the formation of business monopolies and ensure fair competition among businesses). White was also in charge of screening potential judicial candidates. In May, 1961, White faced his greatest professional challenge. He was forced to send U.S. marshalls to stop race riots in Montgomery, Alabama.

President Kennedy chats with Byron White after White took the oath as Deputy Attorney General.

White Joins the Supreme Court

In 1962, Supreme Court Justice Charles Evans Whittaker resigned his position because of health reasons. That left a vacancy for John F. Kennedy to fill. He immediately nominated his friend and supporter, Byron White.

"I have known Mr. White for over twenty years," said Kennedy. "His character, experience, and intellectual force qualify him superbly for service on the nation's highest tribunal."

In those days, the Senate—placed in charge of screening all Supreme Court nominees—did not investigate and question candidates

White testifies before the Senate Judiciary Committee before the committee unanimously approved his nomination.

the way they do now. The Senate Judiciary Committee unanimously endorsed Byron White. So did the full Senate.

On April 16, 1962, Byron White became an associate justice on the U.S. Supreme Court.

When someone joins the Court, many people try to anticipate how the new justice will vote on certain issues. With Byron White's first case, America received a good idea how Byron White would approach his work.

In the case of Robinson vs. California in 1962, the majority of the Supreme Court ruled

Byron White in his robes prior to taking his seat on the U.S. Supreme Court.

that it was illegal to punish someone for drug addiction. But White, even though he was new, disagreed with his fellow justices. He wrote a dissenting opinion stating the reasons for his disagreement. White felt that someone could be punished for addiction because drug use was illegal.

In his dissenting opinion, White showed that he was confident of his opinions, and unafraid to express them. He also showed that he was an independent man who favored strict law enforcement.

He did not believe in using the power of the Court to deal with social problems. Many people did not agree with White's opinion. But he gained the respect of his colleagues and critics.

Defending Individual Rights

hroughout most of his career, Byron White has consistently voted in favor of equality for minorities and women. During his first full term on the Supreme Court, White ruled five times in favor of blacks who were originally convicted by lower courts of trespassing during sit-ins. He consistently voted in favor of school desegregation and busing, and the rights of minorities to seek housing in all-white neighborhoods.

In 1971, White disagreed with the majority of his fellow justices when they decided not to interfere with the city of Jackson, Mississippi, after it closed a municipal swimming pool. Jackson had been ordered by a lower court to make the swimming pool available to blacks as well as whites. But the city refused to obey the order. Instead of desegregating the pool, Jackson decided to close it.

The majority of the Supreme Court thought there was not enough evidence to prove racial discrimination, but Byron White disagreed. Though the pool remained closed, White had clearly displayed his belief in equal rights.

Byron White was also a defender of affirmative action policies for working minorities. (Affirmative action plans are designed to keep a specific number of jobs open for minorities.) Between 1978 and 1980, White voted three times in favor of such plans that were challenged by whites who were seeking jobs given to minorities.

White agreed with the majority of his fellow justices that affirmative action plans were not established to discriminate against whites, but to give minorities and women a better chance to obtain work.

Lately, however, Byron White has been taking more of a conservative approach when it comes to individual rights. It has been increasingly difficult for those in favor of civil rights and affirmative action to find a sympathetic ear from Byron White. No one really knows why he has switched his views. But there is no doubt that Byron White has played a major role in establishing equal rights for minorities and women.

Keeping Big Business in Line

Since the early days of America's economic boom, laws forbidding business monopolies and price fixing have been in force. These laws, called antitrust laws, make sure there is a fair and competitive business environment in America. Such an environment guarantees that companies big and small can prosper. It also keeps alive the American Dream for those who want to share in America's wealth. Throughout his career, Justice White has been in favor of these anti-trust laws.

In the 1960s, White fought hard against the mergers of big companies that would create business monopolies and make it hard for smaller business to compete. In a 1966 case involving a large grocery chain called Von's Grocery, White agreed with the majority of his fellow justices that Von's desire to merge with another large grocer was illegal.

White feared that this merger would allow Von's to control a large part of the grocery market, drive the competition away, and allow Von's to charge what they pleased for groceries.

In another case involving the well-known Schwinn Bicycle Company, White voted in favor of the individually owned Schwinn bicycle shops to sell their bicycles anywhere they wanted. The main Schwinn company wanted to place territorial limits on each of their individual store owners (known as franchise owners). This would make it impossible for franchise owners to sell bikes outside their restricted territory. But Byron White ruled that this requirement was illegal. He felt that the store owners should have "the freedom to dispose of the goods they own as they see fit."

In the 1980s, the majority of the Supreme Court began changing their views on anti-trust laws. It became harder and harder for small businesses to gain favorable rulings from the Court. Many people wondered if Justice White would start changing his views as well, as he did with individual rights. But White has remained a staunch defender of anti-trust laws.

Power to the Police

hough Byron White
has taken a traditionally liberal view on individual rights and antitrust laws, he is conservative when it comes to rights of persons accused
of crimes. Throughout his career, White has
consistently voted against legislation that
would place restrictions on police action. In
his very first case, *Robinson vs. California*, White
agreed with the California law agency that
drug addiction was a crime, even though the
state could not prove that the man, a drug
addict, had actually used drugs in California.

In 1963, White disagreed with the majority of his fellow justices when they ruled that a
written confession to a crime had been
obtained illegally and could not be used in
court to convict the defendant. The defendant
had confessed twice to the crime, but was held
by police and denied phone calls to his wife
until he gave a written confession. White felt
that since the man had already confessed twice
to the crime, the written confession should
have been allowed in court.

The most famous of all Byron White's criminal rights cases came before the Court in 1966. In the Miranda case, the defendant claimed that his rights were violated when police refused to allow him to have an attorney present during questioning.

The majority of the Supreme Court agreed with the defendant. Justice White did not agree. From this ruling, a new set of criminal rights was established. It requires police to give a criminal suspect a warning as to his or her rights about answering questions without the presence of a lawyer.

White believed that statements given by a suspect with or without a warning should be considered legally obtained. He thought that this new requirement would make it more difficult for police to do their job and allow many criminals to go free. "A good many criminal defendants will now either not be tried at all or be acquitted," he said.

Byron White also favors allowing police to search and seize a defendant's property. But there must be good cause for the police to believe something is hidden in the property, or that the property can be used as evidence in court against the defendant. Such opinions have drawn much criticism from civil rights groups. But Byron White remains consistent in his fight to grant more power to the police.

Keeping Church and State Separate

When it comes to separation of church and state, Byron White has consistently voted against the use of religious expression in public matters. In 1963, he sided with the majority of his fellow justices when they voted to ban Bible reading and prayer at the opening of a public school day. White felt that the Bible reading and prayer amounted to government approval of a particular religious view which is forbidden by the First Amendment of the United States Constitution.

As late as 1980, White remained consistent about church and state matters. The state of Kentucky had a law requiring public schools to hang privately purchased copies of the Ten Commandments in every classroom. White once again voted that this law was unconstitutional.

And a year later, White voted that it was illegal for the state of Missouri to require a university to allow prayer meetings in its classrooms. These decisions have been unpopular and are charged with emotion.

Byron White voted to ban prayer in public schools in 1963.

The Right to Privacy

Byron White has consistently voted against governmental interference with the lives of American citizens—particularly when it comes to the marriage relationship. On the historic *Roe vs. Wade* decision in 1973 which legalized abortion, Byron White lashed out at the majority of his fellow justices, calling the ruling "an exercise in raw power." White saw the decision as a major interference by the government into the private lives of married people. According to White, the Court should never have dealt with such a matter.

Since the historic ruling, White has worked hard to chip away at its effect. He has consistently voted in favor of laws restricting the right to abortion. He favors allowing the husband to deny his wife an abortion. And he favors denying minors the right to an abortion without parental consent. White also backs cutting off public funding of abortions.

White has drawn criticism for his views on abortion—especially from women's groups. But White sees the issue as government interference in people's private lives.

The Legacy of Byron White

Byron White may not be considered a great Supreme Court Justice. In all his years as a justice, he has yet to write a majority opinion on a significant issue. Many times when he dissents, he will refuse to give his reasons.

But Byron White's value may be his consistency and his middle-of-the-road views. He has proven to be a balancing power on a Court that, over the decades, has occasionally swung from liberal to conservative. Most importantly, Byron White has defended the Constitutional rights of American citizens.

Glossary

Abortion: Expulsion of a human fetus during the first 12 weeks of gestation.

Affirmative Action: An active effort to improve the employment or educational opportunities of members of minority groups.

Anti-trust Laws: Laws protecting commerce from unlawful monopolies or unfair business practices.

Constitution: The fundamental law of a state which guides and limits the use of power by the government.

Desegregation: Requiring isolation of members of a particular race in to separate groups.

Senate: A governing or lawmaking assembly. The Congress of the United States is the Senate and the House of Representatives.

Separation of Church and State: Constitutional guarantees preventing the government from favoring a specific religion.

United States Supreme Court: The highest court in the United States, which meets in Washington, D.C. It consists of eight associate justices and one chief justice.

Index